Christmas Renaissance

STORIES OF GRACE, BELIEF AND SPIRIT

J. B. Macomson "Jim"

James B. Macomson, DDS
Illustrator: Madalyn McLeod

To Rebecca,

Peace to you this Christmas and for those to come —

ISBN: 978-1-943258-10-9

Published by Warren Publishing, Inc.
Charlotte, NC
www.warrenpublishing.net
Printed in the United States

Profits from this book will be donated to charities.

Dedicated to all those who seek

Table of Contents

Acknowledgment

I send gratitude, appreciation, and thanks to all who were a part in the publication of this book. Also, to family and friends, whose interest and support were an integral portion of the foundation that led to its completion.

Above all, to God, who gave us Christmas: the reason for it all. Let everyone of us acknowledge Him with prayers of humble thanks and praise...

OF CHRISTMAS STORIES

To read is to sense... a most magical, mystical and unexplainable transformation is possible from the written, changing as it traverses through the mind to the heart. The translation from words to feelings is a gift, one of such proportion that confounds and belies comprehension.

Christmas is a season of sovereignty and spirituality, one that evokes an ever increasing accordion of experiences and emotions that can be unfolded, renewed and lived over and over, year after year. How? Because these and many other stories of Christmas, from the inert ink through an ethereal metamorphosis, can bring forth the very marrow of man and the immortal essence of life, the soul...

Read on...

P.S. Short are these... but the hope is that their messages are long and enduring.

The Place

AGE. It had brought him so much but was now beginning to reclaim through insidious ways those things that were once so vibrant. He was an old man now, somewhat slower in step and shorter of sight, but his mind was at its best. Perhaps for the last time he had again returned, had come back to see that which had created such a profound effect on him and his life: The Place. He remembered that day...

It was a time without complicated things — conveniences they are now called — and before the terrible war across the sea. The exercise in survival that is life had been ever so slowly changing for the better. And he was nine years old, secure in health and satisfaction with the world around him.

December. It was here. December meant Christmas. To a nine-year-old, all of this translated into excitement. On that Saturday in that December, he awoke early. Something was different, he felt, on that day as he lay in his bed, under the warmth of a thick comforter. Inside, everything was as it had always been in the past at the beginning of each weekend. The muffled voices of his mother and father could not be understood as they quietly moved about the kitchen. A fire had been built, and there was a freshness about burning wood in that house. He listened. Nothing. Quiet. No, it was something else. The stillness. Yes, that was it. He knew the difference between quiet and stillness even at his young age. But why was it so still? He went to the window, brushed back the curtain, and saw what had caused this feeling. Snow! Everything was covered. There were no boundaries, no definitions other than softness and smoothness. He stopped thinking about the stillness and almost fell down the narrow stairs that took him to the kitchen.

His mother quickly reminded him with her finger to her lips that his baby sister was asleep and not to awaken her. Hot chocolate was the starter, then came the pancakes. Every Saturday. For breakfast. He could never get enough syrup, even though his father reminded him that pancakes are not supposed to float as his always did. And, trying not to hurry, he did, because this was a very special day. He would go for the FIRST TIME with his father to find and cut this year's Christmas tree.

He started running through the snow as soon as he was out of the back door. His father told him to slow down, otherwise he would quickly tire in the ever-deepening drifts. Both father and son were thickly wrapped in their warmest wools, with hats, scarves, and gloves to protect the extremities. Their home was on the edge of a broad expanse of woods, with rolling hills on all sides. These were covered with every type of tree that one could want or imagine. As they walked, the soft snow crunched as it packed under the weight of their feet. No other sounds were heard as the snow continued to fall.

To get where the fir trees stood, on the far side of the most distant hill, the two walked down a gentle slope into a valleyesque meadow now appearing as if a giant white blanket had been thrown over it. How different it would be in four or five months when the rains of spring would come, bringing forth the bluebonnets. His father loved this meadow which also was a haven for blackbirds. But now, smooth and untouched, it awaited the two travelers.

After what seemed a short forever, they started up the first hill. At the top, his father suggested they rest and have a cup of the leftover chocolate that was in the brown thermos. The two shared the still steaming liquid and looked back toward the meadow. Both knew their tracks would be covered by the time they returned in the fading light. But the boy knew his father would find the way home as he always did.

Almost at the top of the last hill, surrounded by majestic evergreens that looked like they had been cultivated and placed just for this purpose, the boy saw it for the first time: The Place. A picture. A painting. Vibrant, soft and alive. In the center of this, beyond all of his dreams of this first trip, was the most beautiful, most perfectly formed tree that would be the center of his Christmas world this year. He shouted as he started toward the tree. But his father stopped him.

No, it would not be this tree, he told his son. In disbelief, the son asked why.

Deliberately and very quietly, his father pointed toward the top of the tree. Nothing. What was he trying to tell his son? Then suddenly, a spray of light snow came from the branches almost at the tree's tip. His father stooped in the snow, now almost knee-deep on the boy, and pointed again. A winter wren was nesting in the tree top. The son insisted that this was THE tree and that the wren could find another.

In the quiet and stillness of that day, the father explained to his son that this bird, this wren of winter, would only and could only survive one winter, one year, and would never return again. Its life-span ran only a year, more or less. And, if the tree were felled, the bird would die because the snow covered all of the soft grasses, leaves, and small twigs needed to build a nest. God had given the bird all the necessary instincts to survive, the father told the boy. Yet He had given the bird only one trip through life, one tour through the seasons. The father said that God had given man a much longer journey on earth, but only one, just as the bird had. But God gave man the ability to make choices. And it must be their choice, the father's and the son's, to pass this tree by, the most perfect one, and give the bird this only winter of its life.

They left The Place slowly and quietly, with the boy looking forlornly back at the tree. Soon another tree was found near The Place. And, alas, the substitute performed much magic in that house on that Christmas.

Only two more Christmases passed with the father, as he was taken early in life by some dread disease. He was buried at the end of that meadow in that spring, under sunshine, with the bluebonnets bending in a soft breeze. As they were leaving, mother, daughter and son, blackbirds flew over them, causing them to look up. After pausing briefly, the mother looked earthward at the freshly cut head-stone. A tear. A smile. Hand in hand, they walked away, on that day, in that spring.

As the years passed, disappointment turned into acceptance regarding that tree found in The Place. Acceptance then yielded to understanding. He found at The Place that it was not the tree that was important, but rather what God had done for all the creatures of His earth and how He had planned such. He had given man everything yet asked so little. And above all, above everything, He had given His Son, the Christ, who, just like the wren, passed through life only once. Christmas. The reason for it all.

It had taken the boy a lifetime to put all of the pieces together, to get the finished picture. Perhaps, he told himself, that's the way God had always intended it to be.

Tears of Angels

THE time was some years after the Second World War; the place was a simple home in a small town in the South. The father had begun a business that was getting by, as most new ones did in those years. Budgets were paramount, as essentials were needed to live and luxuries were distant thoughts.

The house, the home, was situated on a quiet street, with other modest frame and brick structures, all with the nearness that creates a neighborhood. Two large maple trees and three dogwoods were the shade in the summer and agony in the fall... leaves. Boxwoods were guardians of the front steps leading to the small porch. A living room, three bedrooms, one bathroom, and a kitchen... the standard.

Summers remembered were at times brutal, and the home was cooled by a large attic fan which kept the comfort level tolerable throughout with a gentle breeze. Winters were different, as it seemed easier to keep warm than to keep cool in the summer. Radiators, fed by hot water, were in every room, their clanking and hissing a critical part of that warm house.

In the basement, on the natural, dark and damp earthen floor, stood the furnace, thick and white. The "firebox" was fed by coal, which was stored in a big container, about the size of a modern washing machine. And always, its need was to be constantly filled, else the fire would die, and cold would reign. This task was done by the boy and his older brother of a year. Coal was carried in a wheelbarrow from a large pile of finely crushed pieces located some twenty to thirty paces from the furnace. The coal was delivered from trucks and simply dumped through a square wooden door located on the side of the house.

Many a day, the boy and his brother had watched from their windows as the men labored, unloading the coal into the house, just underneath his room.

It was in the winter of his seventh year that it happened. To the boy, as the days became shorter, so did they become colder. That fall and early winter were more severe than usual, and in that house the furnace worked overtime. Working together, the boy and his brother, in coats and sometimes gloves, loaded the coal nightly. Bedtime did not seem early because darkness fell before the sixth hour of the evening, and their sleep came without difficulty.

To a seven-year-old, noises in the night, in the depth of its darkness, were at times ominous. A bear, a monster? Many times he heard them. And, more often than not, he was out of his bed, across the hall, awakening his protectors, those who would shield him from whatever. His parents. The mother would always get up and go with the boy to patiently listen and, if all seemed well, reassure and tuck him back into bed. But the noises that winter were different, and, as they became so frequent, curiosity began to challenge the childhood fear in the boy.

The latter days of December were the culmination of that growing anticipation of the happiest and most joyous of times for the boy, Christmas. The mother prepared all — the tree decorations, the wonderful food — and always made sure that everything would result in the togetherness, the spirit and the love of that time. The father would somehow elevate everyone above the current theme to that of why it was: a gift, the ultimate in God's love, the Birthday, truly from the realms of Glory. And it was his hope that all of this would extend far beyond his family. And from being that steadfast teacher of right and goodness, he became the recipient of what he believed and lived.

Christmas Eve was cold, and there had been some local talk of snow. Once every fifteen years. The boy and his brother had filled the coal container to overflowing, hoping to get two days without work in that cold place so as to enjoy the time to come.

A hot, body-warming meal was the Christmas Eve tradition; the mother always prepared it, never explaining why other than to say she thought everyone needed it. The father said it was something from her distant past and it was her way — no interferences, no questions.

After dinner, everyone, clad in their winter sleepwear, gathered in the living room. The parents told stories and shared recollections from days long since forgotten but remembered at this time of the year. Amazing to the children that mothers and fathers were once children! Then... to bed. The anticipated excitement of the coming day soon subsided, and sleep came unknowingly.

The noise, again, lasting longer... The boy got out of the bed. The curtains on the window of his room were open, and it seemed almost bright on the outside. Stars... Then he saw it: SNOW! The ground was white, clean, smooth. He almost yelled, but that noise came again, distracting his excitement.

Quietly he tiptoed to his parents' room, gently awakening his mother, in turn his father. Not speaking, his father raised himself from the bed, looked out of his window, and put on his clothes, and his coat, hat, and gloves. He quietly went out of the side door, and walked slowly around the house.

As he went, the fresh snow made a gentle crunching sound under his feet. When he arrived at the small wooden door, he saw them: bits of coal, footprints... Was someone taking the family's source of warmth?

Next to the house was a driveway that circled around the neighbor's house, connecting two streets, as the house was on a corner. The path of the footprints followed the depression of the drive. The father saw no one, heard nothing. He followed where someone had recently walked. Then he noticed something odd: the prints were not of the same size nor seemingly even made by the same shoes.

On he walked, up a gentle slope, and finally to a sidewalk. White, everything, everywhere. Except for the tracks left by the stranger... and, every so often, a piece of coal. The steps were much closer together than his, and maybe he would catch the whomever! Around the corner of the yard, onto the sidewalk he hurried.

Then he saw in that early morning darkness, brightened by the snow, a small figure, carrying two small buckets, one of which had tipped over, spilling, yes, the coal. The stature of this figure was small, almost beyond the father's belief. Not more than six years old, he thought, struggling with the two buckets of coal, the mysterious little one walked, stopping frequently to rest and adjust his gloves. The feet: one with a torn boot, halfway opened to the heel, and the other, a shoe with no form. A jacket, with a ripped elbow and tattered collar, was his body warmth. The hat on his head covered only one ear and was sizes much too big as it seemed to be falling off.

Up the hill to the sidewalk, turning and heading down a long sloping hill, the two figures slowly moved. The father remained in the shadows, with a long distance between him and the child. For almost half an hour the two walked, stopped, and walked. Finally, after almost a mile, on that cold, beautiful Christmas Eve, the journey ended for the boy, but another type of journey would begin for the father. The final stop: a ramshackle dwelling with broken windows and patches of weather-paper covering the walls. The boy went inside, to what, the father could only imagine. As smoke began to rise from a single chimney, the father paused and looked one last time. Turning, the father began his long walk home, now with his thoughts as his only companion.

When he arrived at his home, he stopped, looked at everything that was his, and softly, in silence, cried. Human goodness, God-given, somehow unknowingly was firmly his. A simple gift of warmth would always be there for the small stranger and his family; a bit of coal, that was all. A gift from the earth was allowed to pass to some unknown child, but that and more came from God through the father's heart on that very special night. Not the material but the spirit and the feeling created one more rock in the foundation of human kindness and love that the father would give to his children throughout his life.

Always composed, the father needed some minutes before going inside his home. During that time suddenly it began to snow! And gigantic in size, perfect in shape, these flakes floated, almost suspended in that cold air. Slowly they came down, almost not wanting to reach the earth. So thick were they that vision was unable to discern even the adjacent house. Why? Why here, around and on the father? It appeared to be only for him.

Throughout the following years, as age caused the body and mind to change, the boy finally knew the answer to this event: angels. They had been there on that Christmas Eve so many years ago. For the father, they cried in gladness and love, for this small event that changed two lives and lives to come. That snow, so perfect, was the tears, the tears of angels.

Christmas Day was as was expected and more. Yet the father was perhaps more subdued, and his gentle smile seemed to linger a bit longer than usual. Never again would he arise in the darkness to

the scratching and bumping noise in the cold winter nights, for he knew....

Sometime later they stopped, the noises, never to occur again. Ever. He went once again for the last time where he had walked on that snowy Christmas Eve, only to find the place to which the boy had traveled abandoned. Did this poor child, aged beyond his years, ever know what had happened that night? No one knows, but does it really matter?

The son would forever remember the events of that winter, that time, that night. And always at Christmas when he saw snow, he would wonder, are the angels crying for someone?

Belief of Spirit

CHAINS... usually for keeping things in, these particular ones were for getting something out: his car... out of the snow. As he was putting them on the rear tires of his car, he looked at their metallic grey links of steel. His thoughts gathered around them. He remembered: all the times he had put on chains connected past to present. The chains. For the children, then and now. The last time he had performed the task was over there, in 1944, in that war, in the winter of snow and mud, a mixture that prevented movement away from capture or death from a desperate enemy. He was the driver of a truck, the last truck, and, with the help of chains, they had escaped.

Carrying not his fellow soldiers, but children, natives of the contested land. Refugees. Expatriates. Impediments to victory or defeat. Thinly and shabbily dressed, they carried their only possessions: fear and hunger. They were of all ages, brothers and sisters together, others alone. Their faces carried something else: an ever present appearance... a distant nothingness.

Reflected off the snow, the glint of the sun in his eyes focused his thoughts on the immediate project, one that would profoundly change, transform, and elevate the lives of children — not in war, but from its results.

He went back inside his home to rewarm, to say goodbye to his family: his wife, seven-year-old twins, a boy and a girl, and a grandmother. It was the first Saturday in December, and breakfast would be down the express track — table to stomach — and then out to the snow.

As he slowly lifted his foot off the clutch pedal, he heard and felt the crunch as the tires, with their chains, grabbed, dug into, and moved the car in the snow. The drive to the church was but a few miles, time enough to recollect the recent past and what was to come.

For five years, during that war, the needs of the people in this small city had shifted downward: necessities and no excesses. Now they were beginning to recover. But not everyone. There were more than a few families who were now partial families, without fathers, fathers who did not come back, who were buried in those distant places.

He saw a few had already arrived at the church as he drove into the parking lot. Inside, coffee and doughnuts, a church-meeting staple, greeted the arrivals, as always making for a better meeting. About twenty was their number, all men, all from the war, all from their country's service. Coming together to serve again.

The minister opened the meeting with a prayer, not of asking, but of gratitude and humble thanks for what had been given. A man rose, a colonel before and still now a leader. In military style, but with a civil presentation, he gave them the facts: families with children but without fathers were members of their congregation. And it was Christmas. The plan was to match, to pair, the families and their children — those without with those who possessed. The church had a small special fund, discretionary they called it, that would be used. Suggestions were made and questions were asked, as this was the first undertaking of its kind — and many more would follow in years to come.

Children with children. The focus. To treat those in need to the atmosphere of the season. The town would be their source; their hearts would do the rest. These would take those, to experience it all, and to begin to instill the spirit, the reason...

A surrogate father he would be now, yet only for a short time. His new kin were a widow and two children close in age to his own: a boy, six, and a girl, seven. Driving home, with thoughts of the coming days, not of lists of tasks to be done but an agenda of happiness, he smiled.

Lunchtime. An attempt at a snowman, with sticks for arms, small pine cones for eyes, and brown leaves for a mouth, was in the center of his yard. Wet boots on the porch. Inside, just finishing their soup, the children were readying themselves for the afternoon shift of fun. But first, he wanted to talk to everyone of the coming days and of what was to happen. Understanding the differences among people and the reasons for such could be confusing to the young. The simplicity of the known was the key to engaging their understanding, and as he slowly and deliberately built and expanded upon an explanation, he found the key that they could grasp, a symbol, simple and almost universal: the flags.

Everyone knew, even his children: in every home of those who served hung a small flag in a window or on a door, visible for all to see, inside and out. It was a small white square, contrasted by a red border. A star was in the center of the white square: a blue one for the living, a gold one for those deceased. His children understood, not the long history, not the depressing details, but that Christmas would not be the same for some, those of the gold star, as it would be for them. They would go, the blue stars, to brighten Christmas for the gold stars. But to the children, this meant going to the places of toys, looking and buying for their guests. The ways of children — but no, that was not the course that would be taken. For six- and seven-year-olds, the direction of their belief would be guided by the adults, to Santa Claus, the center of a child's world. But beyond the material and the mortal, he was the unbreakable bond connecting man's heart to its source, the spirit of Christmas. He would listen. They believed. He would deliver not only the tangible but the untouchable, the divine, from the realms of its origin: God's Incarnate, Jesus... Christmas.

The much-anticipated day arrived. The father and his two children would go; mother and grandmother would remain at home... holiday things to do. The children talked, sang and drew snowmen on the frosted car windows on the trip to pick up their two guests. Their destination took them past a part of the town less fortunate in its features than theirs: smaller houses, few cars, and unpaved streets.

Finally at the end, the dead end, of one of these streets was the house, that of the family of three. His children had stopped their prattle when they saw it: the flag. The gold star. They looked with forlorn interest at the house as their father got out to fetch the ones from their home. They waited. As he knocked on the door, a bare bulb above his head lighted. The door opened, and they could see the mother smiling and talking. She closed the door, and he returned to the car, opened the car door and told the children to come: they had been invited inside and then would go to town after a short visit here.

The father had not prepared, had not forewarned his children of what they might encounter, although they were aware that some had more than they and some had less. They entered, with undetected hesitancy, a small living room with a sofa and two chairs, neat but worn. An even smaller kitchen could be seen through an open door. Just to the left of the living room ran a four-foot hallway, a bedroom on either side, and, at the end, situated oddly as if an afterthought, a very cramped bathroom. With tongues of granite and eyes opened much wider than normal, the children from the "other side" of town took in the meager surroundings. Finally one asked the children of this house where their Christmas tree was. Their counterparts pointed to a wall behind one of the chairs.

Turning on the one lamp, they pointed to a large picture of a decorated tree. They explained that they did not have enough money for one, but next year theirs would be real, like the one in the picture; they had been saving extra pennies. Under the picture sat a jar containing several coins.

No other decorations were in that house. The father could see his children wanting to speak, to ask about matters in this house. As one started to speak, he held his finger to his lips: a signal not to ask, no more, not now. They always obeyed this silent rule. They would find out later. After explanations to the mother, the children were out the door, heading toward the car. Out of earshot, the secret details were imparted: Christmas Eve. Santa Claus. Belief and fantasy becoming a reality.

As afternoon was giving way to evening, the mixed quintet left for the city.

The town, at least now, seemed to have been built with Christmas in mind. The courthouse sat in the center, with all the stores, shops, a bank, and offices forming the sides of a square, in deference to the giant granite structure of government. Yet all of these structures appeared as simple backdrops to the flowing arrangements of colored lights, with supporting decorations. These would remain shining through the night, while the commercial parts would close at nine o'clock. Plenty of time. But first, food — a meal was in order.

To the cafe they went. People were beginning to gather, but there were vacancies in the eatery. A large booth was their indoor picnic table, and all took their places. A menu with endless selections — too many: these four children wanted everything. With gentle persuasion, the father suggested that, since it was Christmas time, they have the "Christmas Special: Turkey, rice, gravy, candied sweet potatoes, green beans and freshly baked yeast rolls." And pecan pie with vanilla ice cream was the grand finale. He knew it would fit his budget: Adults 75 cents; children 35 cents. His children ate, and their chatter was equal to their chewing. But their guests, the two others, consumed their meal as if it were their first... or their last. With each bite they exuded pleasure as they savored the richness; everything before them was only for royalty, but now it was their lofty culinary pleasure — for the common person, exquisite cuisine.

Finished, full and content, they began the serious enjoyment. They walked and stopped, looking into every window. After the sun's light was gone, the stores were brighter, presenting their visual welcomes. The department store. Santa Claus. Impatience. Normal. A small crowd had gathered in front of this place, a site for most needed things: furniture, appliances, clothing, and household fixtures. Not much was not there. The crowd was watching something in the window, a small screen in a console wooden box: a television. An Indian. The test pattern. Then it changed. A puppet, a marionette, appeared, moving and speaking, "It's Howdy Doody time!" The children jumped, squealed and listened. After some minutes, their curiosity satisfied and affected by the cold, they began to disperse away from the window.

A line was beginning to form inside of the store... Santa Claus. These four children wanted to see him, and tell him. They were still of the age in belief and acceptance that this man would grant their wishes. The visible euphoria of these moments in the sub-culture of wonderment, childhood, was equal in spirit to that of the adults. His children went first, talking and gesturing to Santa, who finished this visit with a smile and "Ho, ho, ho, Merry Christmas!" Then the two without a parent went next. Standing next to the large man in red, they whispered in his ears. His smile disappeared and he looked with question at them. But quickly he recovered and told them his elves would get to work tonight on their request. They stepped down and Santa's eyes followed them, with a distant visual inquiry.

A mental alarm sounded in the father in response to the last two children's encounter and the reaction of this Santa. As the four youngsters wandered toward the toy department, the father quickly stepped up to and spoke with Santa. He murmured a brief explanation about the two; he needed to know their wishes. The Santa told him that they only wanted a picture frame, not the usual

toys. The one they wanted was just like the display model in the mirror, frame and picture department. He said it was gold, a bit gilded, with four small red roses, one at each corner. That was all Santa knew. What the father had thought he could easily do — find out and acquire the Christmas presents for these two — had now become a mystery to be solved, then a task to be fulfilled.

He could not see the children, as they had wandered down the toy aisles. Good. He rapidly, almost running, went to the location of the frame; out of their sight, he saw it. "Not for sale. Display only." The sign told its status. Beyond perplexed, his mind, full of mixed questions, raced in all directions. What? How? Only one week before Christmas....

The direct approach. Always the best tact for children. He would ask these two what they had asked Santa to bring them. Perhaps they would give him more information. Not his children, as he already knew, had learned weeks before, from the lists they had made. As they were leaving the store, he asked them; their answer: it was a secret. Santa was the only one who knew as he was the one who brought what was asked for. Yes. A child's reasoning. They smiled. Looking down at them, an "of course" smile was all that he could muster.

One last stop: the bake shop. As a magnet it drew them in. Cakes, cookies, pastries and the sweet smell of other unknown goodies were all around them. They were drawn to a bright glass cabinet containing only Christmas delicacies. The four were locked onto the gingerbread men. No one asked, but he knew. He held up four fingers. The baker removed four of these elfin designed figurines and, in waxed paper, handed them to him. He passed the little brown confections to the waiting hands. His children began to eat. The other two wanted theirs in a paper bag. Why? They told him they were going to take them home, for later, to share with their mother. No questions. One more. Three into a bag. A hint, a partial glimpse for the grown-up: children in size and years but mature in the spirit... of giving.

Sunday came and church. The widow and her two children would be there, as they were every Sunday. Would a dilemma occur if she asked detailed questions? He was prepared, but he still wondered. They were already there when he and his family arrived. The mother recounted the wonderful evening her children reported; this had been the first for them, ever. Did they behave? Were they polite? How were their table manners? His answer was that he could not have asked for anything better. More thank-yous came from her. Finally, they agreed that the parents would meet while all the children were in school, to finalize "Santa's arrival."

Several days later, they met. The three decided on a schedule, a plan for Christmas Eve, for the implementation of it all. Usually, all of these children were in bed by nine. However, due to their excitement, they would be ordered in at eight. And they knew Santa would not come if they were still awake. The "all clear," the ready signal, would be turning off the front-porch light. Ten o'clock should be safe. There would be no problem for the man and wife, as grandmother was the constant guardian of their two.

Before leaving, the mother humbly expressed her gratitude and appreciation for what the church and they were doing. Her children's joy would be the only gift she would want. Through tears, the anti-freeze of her soul, she spoke and said she only wished her husband, their father, could be here. Just one more minute — she wanted to show them something. She went into her bedroom and returned with a flat white box. She opened the box and unwrapped the contents: a picture, 8x10. It was of a handsome man in a soldier's uniform and a beautiful woman in wedding white, both with smiles that had no end. It was the only one she had of him, of the two of them, and she looked at it often with her children. She would lovingly describe this man who was no more, who was a husband and father. They listened and knew him well, if only through the mother's memory. She wanted to look at it every day, have it for all to see. Comfort and solace it brought. But it was too precious, and unprotected; that was why it stayed wrapped and boxed. She said she would like one day to get the perfect frame for it.

Internal shock almost caused him to blurt it out. A frame! The lump in his throat seemed stuck; he couldn't swallow... A deep breath was a good substitute.

The answer to the mystery he had now, but more difficulty would surely come before that task was fulfilled. That afternoon he returned to the store, to the pictures, mirrors and frames department...The frame! He inquired with a clerk; her instructions were as written on the frame, "Not for sale," and there was nothing she could do.

One last try: the manager. He found him in his office and told him of the church's project. Explaining with sincerity and little short of pleading, he told of this fatherless family, these children and their one Christmas wish. The manager, after a second of contemplation, rose from his chair and told him to follow. They went to the department of the Christmas wish. He instructed the same clerk to get a box for the frame. But — Just get the box, he gently told her. He took the frame, removed the tags, placed it in the box, and gave it to the father. How much was owed? Where was he to pay? The manager told him that this transaction had been completed. Closed. Thanking the manager, the father still insisted on payment; the manager gently interrupted. In a slow and deliberate tone, the manager said it was far and above money, that the cost of the frame had been satisfied, paid in full by the acts of their goodness for others — from him and his people. Bidding each other good-night and Merry Christmas, they parted. He carried the frame; the manager smiled.

Upon arriving at home, he assured himself that all preparations were just about complete and everything ready for the Christmas Eve event. Ah, but not quite. Before going to bed, with concern on their faces and in their voices, his children spoke, frankly, forthrightly, and most pointedly. Could they go back to the store and tell Santa they had changed their minds? But why? They saw and understood, but did not

know the words to explain. What they had asked for themselves they wanted Santa to take to the other two, the ones with almost nothing. He knew. He agreed. A change, a transformation came through revelations in their young hearts that would last their lifetimes.

And go they did, to the store, and visited the Santa. Taking some minutes longer, they talked and were heard. The father watched intently as they were leaving; the Santa looked at him, winked and waved. This St. Nicholas had sorted out the pieces. The three left, to the café and hot chocolate. And another gingerbread man from the bakery. As they walked to the car, the father thought: Yes, this IS Christmas.

Christmas Eve. Eight o'clock. The mother, father, and grandmother all together went to the children's room. Tucking them in, the adults talked of what they, the children, had done. And the children asked the adults if they thought Santa would do as the children had asked. If you believe, it will happen, was the reply. Yes, they did believe. And Santa Claus never forgets the good people — children, especially children. The lights were turned off....

Leaving grandmother and the sleeping children, the father and mother, bundled in their winter's warmest, left for the church. It was nine o'clock. Gathering, packing, and sorting the Christmas gifts, the group of Samaritans, with instructions and directions, were ready to depart on their given routes. Gently stacking the wrapped presents in their car, the couple checked their list and found everything in order. The last, the frame, in a box similar to others, would be just another... non-descript... the children's only wish.

The front porch light was out. Stopping the car, they waited; the front door opened, and, at a wave from within, they began the unloading. Taking the many wrapped surprises inside, the mother of this house began to cry once again. No words were exchanged, but smiles were. A final trip and three stuffed colored stockings were hung over the small fireplace. Footsteps on the front porch? There was one more thing... She opened the front door, and two men of the church brigade came in with it: a tree, a Christmas tree already decorated with lights, tinsel, ribbons, just like in the picture on the wall. All of the presents were then moved under the tree, the frame just one of many.

Man's power, electricity, brought to life the lights of that tree, filling the room with a brilliant myriad of glowing color. But beyond the seen was the unseen: the spiritual power over this and all, everywhere, that brought Christmas through those giving.

The members of the two families and the church men said good night. Through more tears, and fighting disbelief, the mother of the two inside, her words so limited, gave to them her heart's thanksgiving and asked God's blessing for them... always. She would sit and sleep on her sofa, in the midst of the worldly miracle in that room; she would be there when they came in... the children.

Early, just before sunrise, in those two homes, noises. In one, the grandmother was awake first, making coffee, readying a special breakfast. Then came the children, and then their parents. The appearance of so much, so many bright packages under the tree, confused them and looks of disappointment were on their faces.

But had Santa not told them he would give theirs to the other children? The father sat them down and put his arms around them. He told them they had not remembered what he said: Santa does not forget good children, and don't worry, to be sure, he keeps his promises. Still questioning, they asked if it was okay with God. Yes, he answered, because Santa works for God. Finally unencumbered, Christmas joy was theirs.

Across town, on the sofa for a bed, she awoke early. The tree lights almost equaled the sun in the room, creating a luminary kaleidoscope throughout the branches of the tree. The wrapped boxes were as magical fruit that had fallen from its limbs. Shuffling feet and muffled sounds were brief as the two sprang into the room. An enchanted mixture of excitement, astonishment, and elation never before known came over them upon seeing the tree, followed by a different reaction when they saw the many gifts — almost stopping, pointing and whispering... disappointment. They bent down; then on hands and knees they silently began to shift, shuffle and search, as if looking for something lost, or perhaps not even there. Santa forgot, an un-kept promise. Their mother took notice but said nothing. Suddenly, in the middle of the pile, they found it. They held it high. A flat box, wrapped in white, with a painted picture of a sleigh pulled by reindeer and its driver. A simple, small, red tag: "For Mother from Santa." Dancing a three-step jig, carrying the box, they gave it to her. In her lap, she placed her crossed hands on the box. She knew about all the other things, but not about this. Impatience came from the children, to open...now. Unwrapping, lifting the soft paper from around, her eyes saw a dream, a fantasy, and the unattainable was now hers. Emotions, almost overwhelming her, were softened by the adoration of her children's embracing arms. Human happiness could go no higher. Gently pushing them away, she motioned them toward the tree...

As previously arranged, the family of five would travel to visit their new family on Christmas afternoon. Before they could get out of the car, the three were on the porch, waiting. Eight voices simultaneously, in all directions, they fluttered, a song of happiness without music, to each other, to all. Then, children to the tree while adults remained on the porch. The mother told the story of the frame, of how many times of wishful shopping she and the children made, to the place of the frames in that store. Always touching it and telling her little ones how, perhaps, someday, it would be the one... the perfect frame. As she continued with gratitude and, yes, more tears, the father stopped her and motioned to go inside.

Under the tree, with presents, ribbons and paper mixed with arms and legs, the children played. On the small table, under the lamp's light, it sat. The picture in the perfect frame; so much it was, so much it told. Santa had kept his promise. Nothing was even mentioned by anyone of the other request, of the children giving up their desires so two others without would now have. Santa had kept this promise too, remembering.

Darkness came, yet the brilliance of that Christmas Day still remained in that home. Needing, but not wanting, to depart, with embraces and words of deepest gratitude, they left on the journey back across town. The car started and the chains began their labors again.

Night was Heaven's stage; the essence of its endless ebony was a panorama filled beyond infinity with stars and the scintillation of their permanence; their twinkling, as if the angels were winking of God's approval of it all, for the acts of sacrifice and sharing, made meager abundance multiply and everyone was richer that day and forevermore. Belief and spirit were bound in faith; they awoke and coalesced, soaring on God's Grace.

The Cardmaker

WOULD this be the year for him? Too much time had gone by. He was an artist by trade, not through original intent but through the circumstances of life. A cardmaker, a designer, a producer and seller of such things was he. Cards. Everyone used them.

His life was unlike that of most of his peers, but it was good. He had been raised by his only relative, a widowed aunt, as his parents had vanished in his first year, leaving him abandoned. She loved and treated him as the child she never had.

She stretched her meager resources as far as possible, often going without herself in order to make his life the best it possibly could be. Through the church and his aunt's teachings, his foundation in truth and good was firmly established.

Of all the times in his life, the season of Christmas was the ultimate, the best of all, and it was a simple holiday present from his aunt at the age of five that would change his life. This was a box of watercolor paints, a small brush and a thick pad of paper. His early talent astounded his aunt, who often told him it was a gift from God and it should not be wasted. As he grew older, his ability, although self-taught, was refined to something like that of an aged professional. Because of his talent, ability and good grades, he was offered a scholarship to the state university to study art and design. That chance never came because of the war, that war.

He was drafted one month after his high school graduation along with thousands of others his age. And after only six months of training, he was there: the jungles, the rice fields and a culture that no one seemed to understand.

Three months after his arrival, on one of those missions, it all ended for him: an explosion in the trees, accompanied by screams and yells, was that hellish event. He felt nothing — not pain, not well-being, just nothing. He could not move nor could he speak, but consciousness was still with him. Suddenly, a giant of a man lifted him up in his arms and said they must get away as there were more shells to come. The man was Joseph, his friend from the squad of men, all of whom were gone, save these two. Joseph carried and dragged him to the safety of a deep hole covered with downed trees. Another blast and Joseph seemed to fly away.

His memory was like a light switch, off and on, for months in that hospital where the attempts were made to restore him. In his lucid times, he would ask about the fate of Joseph, and the answers were always the same: probably dead, maybe captured, or in rehabilitation somewhere. But they would always promise to keep trying to find out what had happened to this man, Joseph. Finally, he was discharged, as all that could be done for his broken body had been done. Disconnected muscles and nerves caused awkward movement and pain, but determination was his constant companion that would help him to make the most of what was left of his physical self and his life. He was offered employment in business places that hired the handicapped, but his fortitude and pride said no. He would go home.

After a two-day bus journey, he arrived and was surprised to see the minister from the church he had faithfully attended for so many years, who welcomed the crippled one and told him to come and sit, as there was some news that he must learn. He was devastated as he was told that his beloved aunt had passed away while he was in the hospital; people had thought it best that he not be told, due to his fragile condition. Her rental house had been sold, and their possessions were stored at the church. One of the church members owned a small house on the outskirts of town where he could live as long as he wanted. But what to do? One day at a time would be his prescription for living, for it was through his military training and his aunt's teaching that adversity would be overcome.

He went back to the one talent he had, that "gift," as his aunt used to tell him, that of the pen, the brush, the colors, the lines and the figures. But how could he make a livelihood from that? One day in the local drug store, he passed a card display and saw such a variety of shapes and sizes, the notion struck him that he could do this. From his small desk he toiled and submitted samples to the big, nationally known companies. Excellent work, he was told, but they were looking for something a bit different. Discouragement always accompanied the rejection letters, but tomorrow was coming, another day, and he would not give up.

One late November Sunday, as he was leaving church, the minister told him that the announcement cards for the church's Christmas bazaar had not arrived and asked if he could make something on such a short notice. Yes, and he did. His creation caused quite a stir, and later, because of this "emergency job," orders, although small in number, began to arrive throughout the year and in the years that followed. But Christmas was the time that he always looked forward to; there was strength in that season for him, something unexplainable that always uplifted and sustained him, and there would be his concentration.

As the years went by, his success as a cardmaker reached that of a regional star of his profession. His business provided him adequate funds for a comfortable life and travels to the conventions of his trade. He met others like himself, all of whom had similar stories of their day-to-day experiences. There was comfort and a camaraderie in those annual gatherings, and he enjoyed and learned from them. He felt a measure of success there, realizing where he was and from where he had come. He felt he had done all that he was capable of, maybe more. Yet there was something missing — a part of life, a part of succeeding. The final part. Throughout the years, his strength, his daily life, his good deeds, and his faith kept him above what could have been simply the existence of a handicapped man. He would look to that faith, through his God-given talent, to find the last piece.

A fleeting fantasy that occurred to him each year was of winning the National Christmas Card contest. From throughout the nation would come entrants, and only one was selected from thousands. To win meant instant fame and no financial worries for the rest of the fortunate one's life. Yet it was neither the financial gain nor the notoriety that he wanted. In the world of card-making, there was nothing more, nothing left above this lofty pinnacle of being linked in history with one's country and Christian faith. But that was not what was in his heart or his soul but rather the giving back to God, to the world, what had been given to him, his talent, this gift that he possessed. He had made life's journey and this would be the treasure he carried, finally, at last delivered.

That Christmas season, after many months of work, it was ready, the card. An artistic and modern marvel had made this inert piece of paper come alive to tell the story of Christ's birth. A normal-size card it was, with the single word "Christmas" on the front. At the touch of a finger, the card came to life, as it was powered by a battery no thicker or larger than a postage stamp. It was almost like a movie of paintings that portrayed the entire Christmas story on the face of this card. Through his brush and paint, and with the help of modern computer magic, this flat, thin card had a life unto itself. Nothing came close to this, his ultimate effort, his offering of himself.

That Christmas Eve, the night of nights, began with a visit to the local church a few blocks from his home. Snow was falling, with a constant wind that enhanced the overall beauty and feeling for him. His cane crunched in the fluffy accumulation as he walked to the comfort of that sanctuary that would give warmth to his soul as it always did. Carols, candles, and messages of that miraculous birth made his throat tighten as he remembered times gone by. *Merry Christmas*, everyone said, and so did he as the departures to homes began.

Back in his home, he took off his coat, hat and gloves and readied himself for bed. The announcement. It would be decided before midnight and the winner would be known throughout the country by way of the annual presidential message at noon on Christmas Day. He threw one more log into the iron stove that would burn slowly through the night, warming his small house. Under thick comforters, he propped himself on a pillow and looked one last time at his creation, the card. Sleep came quickly, without effort.

How long he had been asleep he did not know as knocking at his door startled him. Who and why on Christmas Eve? He got out of bed and began slowly moving toward the door. Funny, his legs seemed to be without pain this night. Before he opened the door, he asked in a loud voice who was there. *Joseph*, came the reply, the one who had saved him, many decades ago. But Joseph had died in the explosion in the jungle. This had been finally decided as searches in other places had turned up nothing. He opened the door — and indeed it was Joseph, his familiar, dark face glowing! They embraced for a long time, with tears and pats on one another's back. Why? What was he doing here? Joseph said he would explain in the car, for they had to go. But where? Why now of all times?

Joseph explained that the Judge was going to be at the state capital to render the decision for this year's card and his was one of the finalists. Joseph said they must drive and, although the distance was less than an hour, with the snow it would take longer, and they must not be late.

As they drove, he questioned Joseph about his disappearance, death, or whatever happened, and the answer he received was that he, Joseph, had received the best in rehabilitation, almost like a new life. Joseph also seemed to know much about his friend, this cardmaker, and his life after the war. How did he know? Joseph used the old cliché that word gets around. There was a sincere calm in Joseph's voice, so different from that of his military days, as he spoke of those past events.

After a drive that seemed so short in time, they arrived at the convention center.

Inside, there were many people — individuals, groups and even families shaking hands, embracing, and constantly smiling. Then the two men saw him: the Judge. He was about the same as they were in physical stature, dressed in a light, bluish-grey suit. He waved to Joseph to come over, come to him.

The Judge shook Joseph's hand, then that of the cardmaker. It was wonderful to meet him, the Judge said, and told him that he had followed closely the cardmaker's efforts in life. There was warmth in the Judge's handshake and voice that bathed the cardmaker in ease and comfort. All of the cards were winners, the Judge had said, but on this night the cardmaker's effort was so unique, so encompassing, replete with his history, and so created with human experience and love that the Judge had declared this was his time. His was the prize as the winner of this year's Christmas card competition.

As they were parting, the Judge said he was most pleased with the culmination of a sometimes difficult life that had given to all this one lasting gift of love. There would be another prize, he said, and they would meet again.

Never in his entire life had this crippled man, this cardmaker, experienced such feelings of truth, sincerity, contentment, and, yes, love from words spoken by another. As the Judge departed from them, going off into the crowd, gathering those around him, he and Joseph left, walking close to each other without talking, only smiling.

He at last asked Joseph, *Who was that man, the Judge?* Joseph replied slowly that his name was the same as it was when given to him on this night of his birth some two thousand years ago.

It was half-past noon on Christmas Day when the lone policeman arrived at the cardmaker's house. No one had seen him, and there was some concern. The officer had come to check on him and to offer his congratulations as the announcement had come from the president in his Christmas message that the cardmaker's entry had been judged the best, the winner from the nation, based on what his card had depicted.

No response came from continued knocking, so the policeman took out his little device, twisted the lock, and the door opened. He could see the man still propped on his pillow with something in his hand. He walked over toward him, gently calling so as not to startle him. No answer. He quietly shook him. Nothing. In his hands was the card, sparkling, glowing, telling the story of Christmas. Tears flowed from the policeman as he knelt beside the cardmaker's bed, and he knew that, sometime on that Christmas Eve, life had left this man.

The officer did his legal tasks of calling the proper people to begin the business of finality. Before the cardmaker's lifeless form was removed, the policeman thought to himself: if only he had known of his accomplishment before he died....

But, for those who remained in this world, if THEY only knew what the cardmaker now knew....

Renaissance of Hope

THE town... a crossroads at first, grew and thrived from a foundation of work, strength, and the will of its people. It was similar to so many in the foothills of the mountains, as if created from the same minds. Streets of earth, lined with oaks at regimental intervals, gave an ordination of civility in the infancy of pioneer progress. At one end of the main street was the anchor, their colosseum of faith: the church... from baptism to eternity. Of wood, of only one color, white, signifying the purity of its being, its simplicity of design, inside and out, reflected the historical heritage of those rural Christian structures. Crowning the steeple's spire was a cross of brass, affixed as a compass of life that created a moving umbra of its shape upon the ground as the sun moved from horizon to horizon during the hours of day. The parsonage occupied its place on one side of the sanctuary as the cemetery did on the opposite side. Offering some type of pseudo-protection, the picket fences surrounded both. Behind the church, a gentle, sloping hill rose to the highest point for many miles; a place from which the expanse of the countryside and all therein could be seen and was never void of visitors. Nothing would ever be built there; consecrated by the people, the land and the fruits it yielded would be rendered to those in need.

From the church for one-half mile led the artery of life, a main street with a continuum of thriving shops and stores that created a rural emporium of business progress. The last structure, the furthest from the church, almost purposely hidden in self-denial of its existence but grudgingly accepted in its need, was the "Funeral Service." Country-gothic in style, it stood amongst tall, stately pines. It possessed well-tended grounds broken only by a lone, pebble-covered circular pathway; a place to which all would come in their time.

October... shorter days, longer shadows. The winds of fall came, with colored leaves riding invisible rails to scattered and random destinations. The people began preparations, with great anticipation and subdued excitement, for the pinnacle days of their faith: Thanksgiving and Christmas, both of great importance and meaning but with a difference: one of man, the other of God.

The days of winds and, at times, cold rain brought something else: The Diphtheria. Everyone in those times addressed the malady as if it were someone or something of importance. Titular, proper politeness, a rank of honor, and all with morbid respect, were given it in conversation when it came to visit. Yet there was the unspoken, and it carried the absolute, the known of this unwanted guest, an insidious sickness in the young and old that carried many of them to their final days. And so it happened in that town....

It began with a random cough, soreness of the neck, fever. Spreading. As quick as weeds of summer, it emerged, first in one, then in many. It ravaged and raged, this "leather hide," as the Greeks first described the hideous formations in the throat. For some it raced to the heart and other organs of life with fatality marking its finish. It came to others with a mildness of form, with recovery following. But always it came with the question: why was life allowed to some but denied to others? Deep into the town these tentacles of wretchedness dug themselves, leaving almost everyone affected.

Eleven: the final number who were taken, seven of whom had not reached their first decade and four who had passed their sixtieth year. After three weeks in duration, well into November, it was over... yet another beginning... of finality. The needs for so many from so much forced a coming together to face the ultimate in human suffering for those lost and those left. As was learned from those before, the process began. The decision was made to treat the eleven as one as the reasons were equal for all. It would be easier....

To the caretakers of the lifeless some went; to the parsonage others travelled. The aged reverend had seen little rest in the weeks of the disease, and his health had been less than the best for some years;

yet he kept the spirits of the people from drowning in the floods of sadness and sorrow. No answer came after prolonged knocking at his door. Had he not been seen the night before, after bidding good-night to several parishioners? The back door — it was open. They found him, slumped in his rocker, motionless, with eyes fixed, an open Bible in his lap. The number now was twelve. All. A dozen. The same day.

Toleration. Endurance. None was remaining. Physical and spiritual exhaustion had taken over. The lamentations of the people went heavenward, but the need was on earth. Desperation was now at the forefront with the loss of their minister, their connector, the possessor and giver of solace, of assurance and hope. Another was needed... "Seek and ye shall find"....

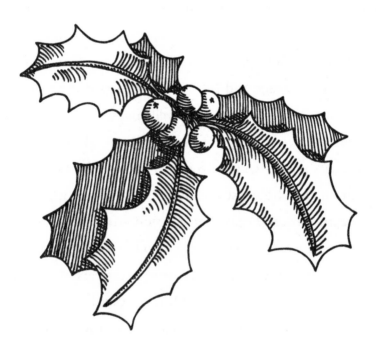

Frenetic tapping with controlled agitation, the fingers pounded. The telegraph key responded. Clicks and pauses. With a rhythm of monotony, of meaninglessness in its sound, it labored. The dispatch was sent and received in nearby towns. The message was brief, profound, and penetrating. "Diphtheria. Minister needed." Responses came, all with regrets and prayers of concern, but all with the same answer: "Unable to help." At the hour of giving up, the machine rattled one last time. From a remote place deep in the mountains, a village — closer in definition to an outpost — it came: "Circuit rider coming. Departing at dawn."

He came not "from" the mountains, but "out of" the mountains, this man, this saddlebag preacher. "From" meant a location in the language of these early people; "out of" was of defining significance, understood, but difficult to explain. It carried a sense, an intuition of knowing the character, the beliefs and the very foundation of the ongoing destiny of a person.

Lincolnesque in stature but with the build and strength of a modern Samson he was. Thirty-four in years, a son of an immigrant minister and wife from the land of the Scots and Irish, he had studied medicine in a New England university for three years, then abruptly left. His letter of resignation was one of gratitude and appreciation, but his calling was greater: returning to the mountains, to his people. From his medical studies and his father's teaching, a blend of a human kind of healing for the body and a sustenance for the soul emerged. Ten years of experience, traveling among isolated habitations, places of pre-rustic beginnings, he perfected and honed his well-received talents. In learning through labors he became a rich man — in knowledge. He would need all of it and more in this town.

A mule of Trojan proportions pulled his wagon, filled with things necessary for the coming task. The journey had taken a full day, and both felt the effects: the muscles of the mule and the mind of the man. As he drew closer, he could see faint glows from the windows, then outlines of people standing in the doorway... of the church.

Introductions, polite greetings, and words of appreciation were exchanged. Late into that first night their meeting lasted. The immediate, the interments and memorials, had already been set — those things, tomorrow. Beyond that existed only incapacitation, even to seek the simplest directions toward normalcy... life interfering with living.

Six horse-drawn carriages, draped in black velvet, carrying two each of the oblong boxes, arrived at the church at noon the next day. They were of polished maple, fine and royal wood, not the usual pine, less than a sarcophagus but more than a casket. "Amazing Grace" played softly, was heard through the opened windows of the church. The cemetery was filled beyond capacity. A cadence of respect sounded as all the names and their ages were slowly called. Bible verses, words of consolation and committal followed. As was the custom, the funeral service always followed the burial; all assembled went inside. The memorial service in the church was a continuation, but with a deeper journey into their faith and the unanswerable: Why? And for them: why the need to go forward, leaving the grief of the present, with the tincture of time helping to heal. After a final hymn, it was concluded. No one spoke as they departed. The services were only words of redundancy for those who listened but compelling for those few who heard.

Saying good-bye to so many loved ones and friends, knowing they would never be seen again, created a pall of despondency, surpassing the predictable and approaching an apocalyptic brink. The circuit rider watched and absorbed. He remained several days more, reassuring that coming good health would return to those still recovering from the disease. And to those many of absent selfhood, of blank existence, showing no apparency to themselves or others, he could only speak encouragement.

His wagon loaded, his mule fed, he began his journey to his home, the mountains. A small group , the few of strength, accompanied him for several miles. Long conversations, questions, answers and opinions were exchanged. By telegram and letter they would keep him informed of the people's condition in the coming weeks. They traveled a few more miles together, then the small group returned to the town.

After only a few days for him, from within and without, came a rejuvenation of energy. The mountains. His home. His people. Yet his thoughts were with those he left, those he knew still suffered deeply. And these thoughts were confirmed with the arrival of the first news, a letter.

In the town, the occurrences were increasing: arguments among friends, the closing of shops and stores, refusal of credit, hoarding of food... The list was lengthy. And, more ominous still: the church... closed. No services. Not even at Thanksgiving. At the letter's conclusion, a request, from a few: could he, would he return? Yes, was his answer, but they must endure a few more weeks... until Christmas. He had unfinished work to complete at his home — but he would come.

The lantern burned long into the December nights as he and his father had deep discussions about the epidemic of non-disease that was slowly and parasitically destroying the human institution of that town. Out of their knowledge and experience, they came to a conclusion: there would be a sequel, a second visit, but with a permeating force, direct and straight to life's essence — their souls.

Christmas Eve... As the sun retreated and gave a peaceful winter gloaming, five riders gathered far from the sight of town: the constable, the caretaker and enforcer of the written and unwritten law; the farrier, a self-taught veterinarian whose knowledge extended beyond animals; the lumberman, who harvested and built; the barber, a gentle, people-appointed counselor, whose ways came from these who sat in his chair; and the book shop owner, a petite woman, a musician of strings and voice, whose life's enlightenment came from the books that were her commerce and the verses of her music.

Five who knew, who had struggled with the circuit rider, five who would continue with this young preacher to give their whole being to salvage and deliver these people, their town, from the self-decimation that had attached itself... and would not let go. They had heard of similar happenings in other towns: a catastrophic event, an upheaval of immense proportions leaving the survivors withdrawn and secluded, surrendering, many of them, moving away in the mind and body to a "safer place," an almost predictable withering, until no substantial functioning of normal life and organized society was recognizable.

They rode toward the mountains, to their meeting with the circuit rider, to forge a plan of purpose. They saw him, his silhouette against a small fire, a large wagon with two mules nearby. Coffee he had prepared beforehand, and the riders obliged his efforts as the hot, black liquid was always a good welcome; they drank with a subdued gusto. No words were needed. Slow, with deliberation and care, he put forth to them what they would do. All in agreement, they prepared to depart. The return journey would take an hour, longer than usual as the wagon was almost overflowing, its contents from the mountains unseen, covered and secured by a large canvas.

The town was dark, and only dim glows of light from behind curtains and shutters were seen... and with no indication of the coming holiday. Almost without sound, they traveled down the main street to the final destination: the church. Quietly, they circled it and the parsonage, to the rear doors. All knew their duties: several into the parsonage, the rest into the church. Their first task was to hang black cloths over the windows — to keep curiosity out and their work concealed. The lanterns were lit, unseen from outside. The large iron heating boxes were stoked and fired, warmth for the night and the coming day. Maximizing their efficiency, they toiled. Finally, finished and satisfied that all was in order, they slept in the few hours of darkness remaining.

Alabaster. Everywhere. A light snow had fallen during the night, and Christmas morning broke with beauty. The six were ready. Nine was the hour: the bells began to ring, and ring, and ring. This was the signal, this constant reverberation of clappers on the bells above the church, for something of great importance. First one, then several, then a large group, they gathered. The church doors opened, and the organ played "Hark the Herald Angels Sing." Then they saw it: a great spruce, a Christmas tree. Center struck. Just below the high altar. Adorned with the berries of winter, dried and candied fruit, handmade sweets, green and red ribbons, and, at its apex, a star of thinly hammered silver. Garlands of cedar hung from the windows, contrasting with the rigid forms of glass. Everything of the mountains, of his people and of their understanding, had come in his wagon. He stood in the pulpit, with his five companions, his collaborators — disciples of the day — directing the people to the pews. No words were uttered; music was the only sound. Astonishment pervaded the congregation as, one by one, they stared, gazing at the surroundings of change. Their faces, underneath their surprise, still held a tedium of fatigue.

The music stopped; he began. The Story: Christ's birth, the angels, the wise men, the shepherds, the manger, and the star. All of it. They had heard it many times on this day in years past. Short in time and words, but with holiness in presentation, it was over. Were quiet whispers, questioning hands and open mouths manifestations of their disappointment? What had been their expectations? The language of their bodies expressed their dissatisfaction: these had not been the desired revelations, but they told the preacher it was finally time, the hour to deliver the maelstrom of awareness to the people, for their lives, The *Gobsmacking*... with reverence.

A term his father had learned from coal miners in England, it was the sudden "smacking" sound that occurred when the sinking "gob" — the velvet sludge that remained after the coal had been removed — gave way. This unexpected loud sound would surprise, shock, and utterly astound those nearby. The word itself was never uttered; rather, it described a method, a technique the older minister used for very special circumstances, to awaken those suffering the darkest realities of life. Comparisons, parables, examples, and alliterations were some of the many means he used — crafted — to impact a change, in individuals and groups, unlocking and transforming without physical touch. Now. It was his time...

Beside the tree, still in the pulpit, he waited, looking at all, looking at none. The organist began the left-right pumping of the foot-powered bellows, bringing the instrument to life. The people exchanged looks again, quizzical at the mystery.

The circuit rider began to sing:

"My hope is built on nothing less..."

A melodic timbre of baritone purity was his voice as it swelled and filled that building.

"I dare not trust the sweetest frame..."

Totally immobile, as if paralyzed, the people listened.

"...In every high and stormy gale,
My anchor holds within the veil."

Something was happening...

> *"...When all around my soul gives way,*
> *He then is all my hope and stay."*

Then came the refrain:

> *"On Christ, the solid rock, I stand,*
> *All other ground is sinking sand,*
> *All other ground is sinking sand"*

Words, music and meaning struck at the innermost of their mortality. They stood. An awakening had begun. They sat.

Speaking with an oratorical eloquence never heard by these people, he continued his endeavors:

> *"Christmas is today, but Christmas is not here, for it has been*
> *excluded — not replaced, but just kept out. So I shall give to*
> *you brief reminders of it and other things.*
>
> *"God gave His greatest gift on this day, His Son the Christ,*
> *and, in doing so, He opened His heaven wider for man. In*
> *Jesus, there was hope...*
>
> *"But here, there is little if any hope, for, as the hymn says,*
> *'When all around my soul gives way'*
> *and truly your souls have given way, and you are 'on sinking*
> *sand.'"*

Their attention and awakening contemplation now belonged to him.

> *"Languor has replaced your life's vitality. Christmas today*
> *is no different for you than the high hill behind us. It's just*
> *there. But, for a few minutes, look at both — the hill and*
> *Christmas...*

"How many have gone to its peak, the hill's? And how many of you have celebrated Christmas?"

All hands were raised... for both questions.

"Why do you and I go to the hill, and why do we celebrate this day? Because something draws us, an invisible attraction that beckons, over and over. Not just for the eyes to see but also for the feeling... the feeling of our spirits. Think now of when you were there on that hill, of the entirety of what was before you, and its effect. It was, is and will be something we cannot put into words — affirmations, expectations, dreams, desires, longings, fulfillment, belief and faith. And so is it also for Christmas.

"And there is one word that embraces it all: **Hope***."*

He paused, and, immersed in his words, they looked within to personal introspection.

"Your small mountain, and Christmas — what they give and what you feel are 'thin places.' A thin place, in Celtic spirituality, is the distance, the closeness, of Heaven and earth. It is an unseen, gossamer veil that separates the two, where the experience is immediate. It is a place where beliefs become reality. A 'thin place' can be almost anything and anywhere: the birthing of a child, the harvesting of a crop, watching the setting sun, every Sunday in this church, and, yes, today, Christmas.

"It is man's reverent awe of God's magnificent wonders...

"You have touched the edge of Heaven; let it continue until

your eternity, when you pass the veil.

"So on this Christmas Day, let us reopen our hearts and allow the gift, hope, to return. Let us learn to live and love again."

An old man, in the corner, on the last pew, stood. Alone, he began to slowly clap his hands. Then everyone followed, and, in unison, they applauded and applauded. Finally, with a gentle nod of appreciation from the pulpit, he held his hands in the air and then moved them downward, the silent signal to sit. The organ began the introductory bars to "Joy to The World" — a final musical uplifting.

In the rear, a single bell began to ring. The people turned toward the entrance; the five were there. Down the center they rolled carts, a linear carousel filled with festive foods, brought the evening before in that wagon with the tree, from the mountains, from his people. In the parsonage, during the night, a few had prepared it for the many. The people's faces glowed; they began conversations, and a restrained relaxation moved among them. The totality of his efforts was taking hold. A blessing he gave, then the Christmas manna. Throughout the remaining hours, until early evening, this awakening, this renaissance of hope was reborn in these people, in that church, on that Christmas Day.

He stayed that night in the parsonage, with cautious satisfaction inducing his sleep. The next morning, the five came to see him to the edge of town, arriving as agreed. One suggested they visit the church one last time... to reflect. The six climbed the steps and opened the doors. The unexpected — taken aback, the circuit rider, in an almost speechless stupor, saw it: the sanctuary... filled to standing. Now he would receive something he gave: a return *gobsmacking* of sorts.

With all eyes and faces now glowing with smiles in his direction, the five and the flummoxed one, walked to the front. A chair for him. Everyone could see. The bookshop owner, the diminutive lass, lifted her mahogany guitar and a song, a Scottish farewell. She began:

> *"Safely o'er the land ye go,*
> *He'rts will a'most break in twa*
> *Should ye nae come back again.*
> *Will ye no' come back again?*
> *Will ye no' come back again?*
> *Better lo'ed ye canna be*
> *Will ye no' come back again?"*

Her voice, a musical rainbow, arched in that church, over and above all, with staying sweetness.

Without invitation or request, and without hesitation, everyone there began singing the last lines, *"Will ye no' come back again?"* They sent to him a resounding, humble choral exhortation, supplication and plea. He rose from his chair; with a swelling heart, he saw through his tears, their tears — truly, a "thin place." With arms crossed and clutched to his chest, he bowed to them, to their rekindled faith. When the last note sounded and the last word was sung, there was total quiet.

They waited.

He responded... *"Aye."*

Back home with his father, he recounted the last days in the town. Of miraculous nature, lives in grief-caused hibernation were stirred from the dregs of their great tragedy. On Christmas Day. Because of God's gift. All of it. Further into their philosophies they delved... about the town, its people, what had occurred, loss of life's direction, and how they were returned. They both realized the reasons and that the cure was almost complete... almost.

Both the father and son knew what had to come: the final nail, the permanent setting of the corner stone. His last journey: he would ride the circuits no more. He would go back to his final calling... in perpetuity, to that town. They would now also become his people.

His permanent homecoming lasted the next forty years. The parsonage was home for him and eventually for his family. The bookstore owner — the bonnie singer, one of the five — and he became mutually smitten. A year they courted. They were THE item of community giddiness. Marriage. Three children. Together, this family and the town continued in prosperity. Yet every Christmas they remembered, each and all, that day, their first Christmas, their beginning.

He remains there even now, but on the other side of the church. Above his name on a polished granite headstone reads an inscription: "Our hope was built on nothing less"; and below his life's duration, another: "All other ground was sinking sand."

CPSIA information can be obtained at www.ICGtesting.com
Printed in the USA
BVOW08*2013021115

425304BV00001B/2/P